The Office Struggle

Empowering Solutions for Handling Work Jerks with Confidence

Victor M. Berta

copyright massage

All right reserved. No part of this publication may be reproduced, distributed, or transmitted in any form or by any means, including photocopying, recording, or other electronic or mechanical methods, without the publisher,except in the case of brief quotation embodied in critical reviews and certain other noncommercial uses permitted by copyright law.

Introduction
CHAPTER ONE
Understanding Work Jerks:
    Identifying Problematic Behaviours
CHAPTER TWO
The Impact of Work Jerks on Workplace Culture and Morale
CHAPTER THREE
Emotional Intelligence:
    Managing Your Responses to Work Jerks
CHAPTER FOUR
Constructive Communication:
    Responding Effectively to Difficult Personalities
CHAPTER FIVE
Setting Boundaries:
    Maintaining Professionalism with Work Jerks
CHAPTER SIX
Conflict Resolution Strategies for Dealing with Work pulls
CHAPTER SEVEN
Building a Supportive Work Culture:
    Countering Toxicity
CHAPTER EIGHT
Leadership's Role in Addressing Work Jerks and

Creating a Respectful Environment
CHAPTER NINE
Recognizing and Handling Passive-Aggressive Work Jerks
CHAPTER TEN
Stress Management:
    Coping with Work Jerks' Impact on Your Well-Being
CHAPTER ELEVEN
Cooperation Tactics:
    Strengthening Unity in the Face of Work pulls
CHAPTER TWELVE
Turning Challenges into Opportunities:
    Lessons from Success Stories
CHAPTER THIRTEEN
Mediation and Intervention:
    Facilitating Dialogue to Address Work Jerks
CHAPTER FOURTEEN
Legal Considerations:
    When Workplace Conflict Requires Professional Assistance
CHAPTER FIFTEEN
Transitioning and Moving On:
    Evaluating Your Career Choices in the Face of Work Jerks
CHAPTER SIXTEEN
Success Stories:
    Overcoming Work Jerk Challenges

Introduction

The Office Struggle - Navigating Challenges and Thriving in the Workplace

Welcome to "The Office Struggle," a book that delves into the complexities of the modern workplace and equips you with the tools to handle its challenges with grit and determination. In this fast-paced world, where careers are formed and dreams are realised, the workplace can be both a source of fulfilment and an arena of struggle. From dealing with demanding bosses to managing difficult colleagues, the hurdles we face in our professional lives can be daunting.

"The Office Struggle" is not just a recounting of workplace woes but a guide to turn these challenges into opportunities for growth and empowerment. Within these pages, we will explore the various aspects of the office environment, shed light on the intricacies of workplace dynamics, and provide practical strategies to help you overcome obstacles and thrive.

In the first chapters, we will address the usual challenges faced in the office setting. We will delve into the complexities of dealing with work jerks - those people whose negative behaviour can create toxic work environments. Understanding their motivations and how to respond successfully will be a cornerstone of developing resilience in the face of adversity.

Next, we will explore the effects of workplace conflicts on morale and productivity. Conflict is a natural part of human interaction, but we will provide you with tools to handle these situations constructively, promoting understanding and collaboration.

Additionally, "The Office Struggle" will delve into the importance of keeping professionalism in the face of challenges. We will cover strategies for successful communication, emotional regulation, and setting boundaries to safeguard your integrity in the workplace.

Moreover, we recognize the significance of work-life balance and will provide advice on how to find harmony amidst the demands of the professional world.

As we progress through the chapters, you will meet inspiring success stories and testimonies from individuals who have conquered the office battle. These accounts will showcase how resilience, perseverance, and the right attitude can lead to triumph even in the most trying situations.

Now, we offer a call to action to you, our reader. Embrace "The Office Struggle" not as an impediment but as a chance to grow, learn, and become a stronger, more empowered professional. Utilise the insights, strategies, and knowledge shared in this book to foster a thriving and harmonious work environment.

Embrace the challenges that come your way, for they are stepping stones to your personal and professional growth. Engage in open conversation, seek support from colleagues, and never hesitate to seek professional assistance if needed. You have the power to shape your job experience and foster a positive effect on your colleagues and the organisation as a whole.

May "The Office Struggle" be your companion in overcoming obstacles, finding balance, and gaining success in the workplace. By navigating the intricacies of office relationships with wisdom and strength, you will emerge as a resilient and empowered professional, ready to seize the opportunities that lie ahead.

Get ready to start on a journey of growth and transformation - together, let's conquer "The Office Struggle" and pave the way to a fulfilling and thriving career.

CHAPTER ONE

Understanding Work Jerks:

Identifying Problematic Behaviours

In the intricate geography of the plant, it's important to be apprehensive of problematic behaviours that can produce pressure, hinder productivity, and undermine the overall work terrain. relating these behaviours beforehand is pivotal to handle conflicts instantly and cultivate a healthy plant culture. By feting and understanding these problematic behaviours, individualities and groups can take visionary measures to minimise their impact and promote a positive and productive atmosphere.

1. Aggressive Communication One of the most egregious problematic behaviours is aggressive communication. This includes crying, using obnoxious language, and engaging in particular attacks during addresses or meetings. Aggressive agents frequently dominate conversations, making it challenging for others to partake their views and ideas freely.

2. Undermining Associates Some people engage in behaviours aimed at undermining the sweats and accomplishments of their associates. This can manifest in colourful ways, similar as spreading rumours, taking credit for others' work, or designedly withholding information.

3. Discourteous station A discourteous station is characterised by dismissive or condescending conduct towards associates or inferiors. This can produce a hostile work atmosphere and negatively impact platoon morale.

4. Lack of Responsibility When people refuse to take responsibility for their conduct or

miscalculations, it can lead to a breakdown in trust and cooperation. Avoiding responsibility can hamper progress and make it delicate to bandy and amend issues.

5. Tattling and scuttlebutt Mongering sharing in gossip or spreading rumours can produce a poisonous work terrain, eroding trust and causing gratuitous pressure among associates.

6. Passive- Aggressive Behaviour Passive-aggressive people may express hostility laterally through affront, backhanded respects, or subtle acts of resistance. This geste
 can be gruelling to defy, but it's essential to address to keep a healthy plant dynamic.

7. Micro-Management Constantly micromanaging associates can produce a sense of frustration and disempowerment, undermining workers' confidence and provocation.

8. Inordinate Negativity Pervasive negativity can bring down the general morale of the

platoon and hamper productivity. Constantly dwelling on problems without giving results can be ineffective.

9. Bullying or importunity Plant bullying and importunity, whether verbal, physical, or emotional, are serious problematic behaviours that can have severe effects on the well- being of affected individuals.

10. Lack of Collaboration Refusing to unite with others or banning certain platoon members from addresses can hamper progress and foster a divisive atmosphere.

Feting these problematic behaviours is the first step towards addressing and settling problems in the plant. It's important to note that individualities may show a combination of these behaviours, and the inflexibility may vary across different situations. In some cases, these behaviours might be unintentional, driven by solicitude, instability, or a lack of mindfulness.

To address problematic behaviours effectively, it's pivotal for companies to promote open communication, give conflict resolution training, and establish clear programs and guidelines. Encouraging feedback and anonymous reporting styles can also empower workers to speak up when they observe similar behaviours.

individuals can play an active part in relating and addressing these behaviours by exercising emotional intelligence, setting limits, and promoting empathy and respect. Having formative exchanges with associates, giving feedback, and seeking support from advanced-ups or mortal coffers when necessary can help address conflicts in a positive and productive way.

In conclusion, relating problematic behaviours in the plant is important for creating a harmonious and probative work terrain. By fitting these behaviours beforehand, people and organisations can take a visionary way to address conflicts, promote open communication,

and produce a culture of respect and collaboration. Eventually, a plant that values positive behaviours and laboriously addresses problematic bones
 can thrive, leading to better productivity and hand happiness.

CHAPTER TWO

The Impact of Work Jerks on Workplace Culture and Morale

In every workplace, the presence of individuals with disruptive and toxic behaviours, generally referred to as "work jerks," can have a profound effect on the overall workplace culture and employee morale. These problematic personalities can cri jerks in the workplace is crucial for organisations to take effective measures to handle and mitigate these negative effects.

1. Decline in Employee Morale: Work jerks create an environment of negativity and hostility, which can significantly affect employee morale. Constant criticism, demeaning remarks, and a lack of respect for hard work can lead to feelings of demoralisation and reduced motivation among team members.

2. Decreased Job Satisfaction: Employees who have to deal with work jerks on a daily basis are likely to experience a decline in job satisfaction. Feeling unsupported, undervalued, or constantly stressed due to these personalities can lead to a lack of excitement for work and a diminished sense of fulfilment.

3. Impact on Team Collaboration: A healthy workplace atmosphere encourages collaboration and effective teamwork. However, work jerks can disrupt this dynamic by causing division and mistrust among team members. As interpersonal conflicts arise, cooperation and dialogue suffer, hindering progress on projects and tasks.

4. High Turnover Rates: The presence of work jerks can lead to higher employee turnover. When individuals feel constantly mistreated or unsupported, they are more likely to seek employment elsewhere, resulting in a loss of valuable talent and increased recruitment costs for the company.

5. Stress and Burnout: Working in a setting with work jerks can be emotionally draining and stressful. The constant tension and fear of confrontation can lead to burnout and negatively impact workers' mental and physical well-being.

6. Reduced Creativity and Innovation: A positive work environment promotes creativity and innovation, as employees feel comfortable sharing ideas and taking risks. However, when work jerks rule the workplace, individuals may be hesitant to speak up, leading to a stifling of creativity and a lack of fresh perspectives.

7. Employee Disengagement: As workers face challenging interactions with work jerks, they

may disengage from their work or adopt a "just-getting-by" attitude. This disengagement can further hamper productivity and hinder the organisation's general performance.

8. Erosion of Trust: Trust is a basic element of a healthy work environment. Work jerks can erode trust among team members by engaging in dishonest or manipulative behaviour, making it difficult for workers to collaborate effectively.

9. Negative Reputation: A workplace with a reputation for harbouring work jerks may find it challenging to attract and keep top talent. A negative impression of the organisational culture can deter potential candidates and affect the company's brand image.

10. Impact on Organisational Goals: The combined impact of work jerks on workplace culture and morale can ultimately hinder an organisation's ability to achieve its goals. Productivity may decline, teamwork may suffer, and total performance may be compromised.

To address the effect of work jerks on workplace culture and morale, companies must prioritise open communication, establish clear policies against toxic behaviours, and invest in conflict resolution training. Encouraging a culture of respect, empathy, and collaboration can help counter the negative effects of work jerks and promote a more positive work environment.

In conclusion, work jerks can greatly impact workplace culture and employee morale. The detrimental effects include decreased job happiness, reduced collaboration, high turnover rates, increased stress, and diminished innovation. Organisations must take proactive steps to handle these behaviours and build a supportive and respectful work environment. By promoting a positive workplace atmosphere, businesses can enhance productivity, foster employee satisfaction, and build a strong and cohesive team.

CHAPTER THREE

Emotional Intelligence:

Managing Your Responses to Work Jerks

Dealing with work jerks in the workplace can be challenging, but how we react to their behaviour plays a significant role in maintaining our well-being and productivity. Instead of reacting emotionally, it is important to manage our responses with emotional intelligence. By developing self-awareness, empathy, and assertiveness, we can effectively handle interactions with work jerks while protecting our emotional well-being and keeping a positive work environment.

1. Self-Awareness: Recognizing Triggers and Emotional Reactions

Self-awareness is the basis of managing responses to work jerks. Take the time to understand your emotional triggers and how you usually react to challenging situations. Being aware of your emotional responses allows you to anticipate potential conflicts and proactively choose how you respond.

2. Practising Emotional Regulation: Maintaining Composure in Tense Situations

When faced with work jerks, it is common to feel frustration, anger, or stress. Practising emotional regulation techniques, such as deep breathing or taking a short break, can help you keep composure and respond calmly instead of reacting impulsively.

3. Cultivating Empathy: Understanding the Work Jerk's Perspective

Empathy includes putting yourself in the other person's shoes and trying to understand their perspective. While it may be challenging to empathise with work jerks, doing so can offer insights into their motivations and help you react with more patience and understanding.

4. Avoiding Escalation: Choosing Productive Responses

Engaging in arguments or retaliating against work jerks can escalate disagreements and worsen the situation. Instead, choose productive responses, such as asking for clarification, using "I" statements to express your feelings, or suggesting solutions to address problems constructively.

5. Setting Boundaries: Protecting Yourself from Toxic Interactions

Establish clear limits with work jerks to protect yourself from emotional harm. Politely but firmly assert your limits and let them know what behaviour is unacceptable. Consistently enforcing these limits can deter further problematic behaviour.

6. Seeking Support: Turning to Colleagues or Managers for Help

Don't hesitate to seek help from colleagues or managers if you find it challenging to manage interactions with work jerks on your own. They may offer insights or provide a different view on the situation.

7. Emotional Detachment: Not Taking Their Behavior Personally

It's crucial to realise that work jerks' behaviour is often a reflection of their own issues and not a reflection of your worth or abilities. Practising emotional detachment can prevent their actions from affecting your self-esteem.

8. Focusing on Solutions: Steering Conversations Toward Resolutions

Instead of dwelling on the negativity of work jerks, focus on finding answers to conflicts. Keep talks goal-oriented and steer discussions toward resolving issues and improving the work environment.

9. Building a Supportive Network: Surrounding Yourself with Positive Influences

Create a support network of workers or friends who can offer encouragement and advice. Having a positive influence outside of work can provide you with a place to vent frustrations and gain valuable insights.

10. Reflecting on Personal Growth: Seeing Challenges as Opportunities

View interactions with work jerks as chances for personal growth and development. Reflect on how you've handled past situations and find places for improvement. Embrace challenges as chances to improve your emotional intelligence and resilience.

In conclusion, managing responses to work jerks takes emotional intelligence, self-awareness, and assertiveness. By understanding your emotional triggers, practising empathy, and focusing on constructive solutions, you can handle interactions with work jerks successfully. Prioritising emotional well-being and cultivating a positive work environment will not only benefit you but also add to a healthier workplace culture for everyone involved.

CHAPTER FOUR

Constructive Communication:

Responding Effectively to Difficult Personalities

Dealing with difficult personalities, also known as work jerks, in the workplace requires skillful and constructive conversation. Responding effectively to these individuals can help diffuse conflicts, keep professional relationships, and foster a more positive work environment. By employing active listening, assertiveness, and conflict resolution skills, you can navigate challenging interactions with difficult personalities while upholding your integrity and mental well-being.

1. Active Listening: Hearing Beyond the Words

Active listening is a fundamental aspect of successful communication. When dealing with difficult personalities, focus on truly getting their worries and perspectives. Avoid interrupting or making assumptions, and paraphrase their statements to ensure clarity and show that you are fully engaged in the conversation.

2. Remaining Calm: Managing Your Emotions

It is natural to feel frustrated or upset when dealing with difficult personalities, but keeping composure is important for effective communication. Take deep breaths, practice mindfulness, and be aware of your emotional state to react thoughtfully and rationally.

3.   Avoiding   Defensiveness: Staying Open-Minded

Difficult personalities may be critical or aggressive, leading you to become defensive. Instead, try to stay open-minded and focus on understanding their underlying concerns. Avoid taking their comments personally and try to see their view without feeling attacked.

4. Using "I" Statements: Expressing Your Feelings Assertively

When addressing problems with difficult personalities, use "I" statements to express your thoughts and observations. For example, say "I feel disrespected when..." instead of "You always do this..." This method takes ownership of your emotions and avoids acting accusatory.

5. Seeking Clarification: Asking for Specifics

If a difficult personality makes vague or unclear statements, seek clarification to ensure you understand their goals or concerns fully. Asking questions can prevent misunderstandings and help you address the root of the problem more effectively.

6. Addressing Behaviours, Not Personalities: Staying Focused on Actions

When giving feedback or addressing problematic behaviours, focus on specific actions rather than attacking the person's character. Addressing behaviours directly allows for a more constructive and less personal conversation.

7. Remaining Professional: Avoiding Escalation

It's crucial to keep professionalism when dealing with difficult personalities. Avoid resorting to name-calling or participating in personal attacks, as this can escalate conflicts and make resolution more challenging.

8. Proposing Solutions: Working Towards Resolution

While addressing issues with difficult personalities, suggest practical ways to resolve conflicts or improve the work environment. Be open to compromise and collaboration, showing a willingness to find common ground.

9. Knowing When to Walk Away: Recognizing Unproductive Interactions

Not all contacts with difficult personalities may lead to resolution. If a talk becomes unproductive or hostile, consider stepping away temporarily and revisiting the problem later when emotions have cooled down.

10. Seeking Mediation: Involving a Neutral Third Party

If efforts to settle conflicts directly with a difficult personality have been unsuccessful, consider involving a neutral third party, such as a manager or human resources representative, to mediate the discussion.

11. Documenting Incidents: Keeping a Record

Keeping a record of problematic events with difficult personalities can be helpful if further action or intervention becomes necessary. Document dates, times, and specifics to back your claims and provide context.

12. Knowing Your Boundaries: Setting Limits

Establish clear limits with difficult personalities to protect your well-being and keep your professionalism. Communicate your boundaries firmly and repeatedly to deter problematic behaviours.

In conclusion, responding successfully to difficult personalities in the workplace takes constructive communication and conflict resolution skills. Active listening, emotional regulation, assertiveness, and finding resolution through open dialogue are important components of managing interactions with work jerks. By staying focused on behaviours, proposing solutions, and keeping professionalism, you can navigate challenging situations while promoting a more positive and respectful work atmosphere.

Remember that dealing with difficult personalities is a skill that can be honed over time, adding to your personal growth and resilience in the face of workplace challenges.

CHAPTER FIVE

Setting Boundaries:

Maintaining Professionalism with Work Jerks

Dealing with work jerks in a professional way is crucial to uphold your own integrity and foster a positive work environment. While it can be difficult to interact with challenging personalities, maintaining professionalism is important for promoting effective communication, preserving your image, and minimising the impact of their behaviours. By setting limits, focusing on your own conduct, and utilising conflict resolution skills, you can navigate interactions with work jerks while demonstrating grace and keeping your professionalism.

1. Setting Boundaries: Defining Acceptable Behaviour

Establish clear limits with work jerks to protect yourself from emotional harm and unprofessional conduct. Politely but firmly communicate your limits and standards, making it clear what behaviours are unacceptable.

2. Avoiding Emotional Reactivity: Staying Composed

When faced with work jerks' provocative behaviour, resist the temptation to respond emotionally. Maintain your composure and approach encounters with a level head to avoid escalating conflicts.

3. Focusing on Professionalism: Prioritising Your Values

Keep your focus on your professionalism and beliefs rather than engaging in counterproductive behaviour. Demonstrating your dedication to professionalism sets a positive example for others and emphasises the importance of respectful conduct.

4. Practising Emotional Intelligence: Understanding Your Emotions

Cultivate emotional intelligence to spot and manage your own emotions when dealing with work jerks. Understanding how you feel in these situations allows you to respond thoughtfully and not react impulsively.

5. Listening Actively: Hearing Beyond Difficult Personalities

Active listening is important in any professional interaction, including those with work jerks. Engage in attentive listening, trying to understand their perspectives and concerns, even when their communication style may be challenging.

6. Focusing on Facts: Addressing Behaviours, Not Personalities

When giving feedback or discussing conflicts, focus on specific behaviours or actions rather than attacking the person's character. This method keeps the conversation objective and avoids personal attacks.

7. Choosing Constructive Responses: Proposing Solutions

Respond to work jerks with constructive and solutions-oriented conversation. Offer ideas for resolving conflicts or improving the work environment, showing your commitment to problem-solving.

8. Not Taking It Personally: Understanding Their Issues

Work jerks' behaviour is often a reflection of their own issues and insecurities rather than a straight judgement of your skills. Avoid taking their comments personally and keep perspective on their behaviour.

9. Seeking Support: Engaging Colleagues or Superiors

Don't hesitate to seek support from colleagues or bosses when facing difficult personalities. Sharing your experiences and seeking advice can provide a fresh viewpoint and potential strategies for handling these interactions.

10. Maintaining Professional Distance: Avoiding Personal Involvement

While working with difficult people, keep a professional distance to minimise emotional entanglement. Focus on your job responsibilities and collaborative efforts, keeping personal issues separate.

11. Practising Assertiveness: Standing Up for Yourself Professionally

Be assertive when discussing problematic behaviours or setting limits with work jerks.

Express your concerns boldly and professionally, without becoming aggressive or passive.

12. Knowing When to Disengage: Recognizing Unproductive Interactions

Some conversations with work jerks may become unproductive despite your efforts. Recognize when it's best to disengage temporarily and revisit the problem later when emotions have cooled down.

In conclusion, keeping professionalism with work jerks is essential for preserving your integrity and promoting a positive work environment. By setting limits, focusing on your conduct, and practising emotional intelligence, you can navigate challenging interactions with grace and composure. Remember that professionalism is a reflection of your values and dedication to a respectful and collaborative work environment, even in the face of challenging personalities.

CHAPTER SIX

Conflict Resolution Strategies for Dealing with Work pulls

When dealing with work pulls in the plant, conflicts are nearly guaranteed. Still, resolving these conflicts successfully is pivotal for keeping a positive work terrain and fostering productive connections. Conflict resolution strategies help handle issues with delicate personalities, support open communication, and find common ground.

By approaching conflicts with empathy, active listening, and a focus on formative results, you can handle relations with work pulls more effectively and promote a healthier work terrain.

1. Approach Conflicts Calmly Embrace Emotional Regulation
When brazened with conflicts involving work pulls, start by regulating your passions. Take deep breaths and stay calm to help replying impulsively. feelings can cloud judgement and hamper effective communication, so keeping countenance is crucial.

2. Choose the Right Time and Place Set Up a Neutral Setting
Schedule a private and neutral place to address conflicts with work pulls. A one- on- one discussion in a quiet and comfortable place allows for open dialogue without distractions or pressure from associates.

3. Use" I" Statements Communicate Your passions

Employy" I" statements to describe your passions and worries without sounding accusatory. For illustration, say" I feel uncomfortable when." rather than" You always make me feel."

4. Focus on Specific Behaviours Avoid Generalisations

rather of making broad generalisations about the work haul's geste

, concentrate on specific cases or conduct that have been problematic. Addressing specific behaviours allows for a more targeted and formative discussion.

5. laboriously hear Understand Their Perspective

Engage in active listening to understand the work haul's view and enterprises completely. Give them the chance to express themselves without interruptions, icing they feel heard and valued.

6. Seek Common Ground Identify Shared Interests

Look for areas of participated interest or collective pretensions with the work haul. By relating participating objects, you can work together towards a resolution that helps both parties and the business.

7. Avoid condemn and Defensiveness Foster a cooperative Atmosphere

Blaming and getting protective during disagreement resolution can hamper progress. rather, concentrate on cooperative problems-working and changing results that meet everyone's requirements.

8. Be Open to Feedback Encourage Honest Communication

Be open to feedback and judgement from the work haul. Encouraging honest communication builds trust and may show perceptivity that can lead to resolution.

9. Use Mediation If Necessary Involve a Neutral Third Party

still, consider involving a neutral third party, similar as a middleman or administrator, If conflicts continue or come ungovernable.

10. Propose Formative results Offer Practical Recommendations

When addressing conflicts with work pulls, suggest practical results that address the root causes of the issue. Be open to concession and show an amenability to work together to find judgments .

11. Follow Through on Agreements Maintain Responsibility

Once judgments are made, ensure that both parties commit to the agreed- upon conduct. Following through on agreements shows responsibility and fosters a feeling of trust.

12. Learn from the Experience Reflect and Ameliorate

Every conflict resolution offers an occasion for particular growth and literacy. Reflect on the experience and consider how you can ameliorate your dialogue and conflict resolution chops.

In conclusion, conflict resolution strategies are pivotal for dealing with work pulls successfully and fostering a positive work terrain. By addressing conflicts with empathy, active listening, and a focus on formative results, you can bridge the gap between delicate personalities and find common ground. Resolving conflicts in a regardful and cooperative way adds to a healthier work terrain, bettered cooperation, and increased overall productivity.

CHAPTER SEVEN

Building a Supportive Work Culture:

Countering Toxicity

Toxicity in any setting, whether it be the workplace, social circles, or online communities, can have a detrimental effect on individuals' well-being and the overall atmosphere. Countering toxicity includes actively addressing negative behaviours and supporting a culture of respect, empathy, and constructive communication. By recognizing the signs of toxicity, setting limits, and fostering positivity, we can create healthier environments where people can thrive and grow.

1. Recognizing Toxic Behaviours: Identifying the Red Flags

The first step in countering toxicity is being able to spot the signs of negative and harmful behaviours. These may include constant criticism, gossiping, spreading rumours, and participating in passive-aggressive actions. Being aware of these red flags helps us to address them promptly.

2. Setting Boundaries: Protecting Yourself

Establishing clear boundaries is important when dealing with toxic individuals. By putting limits on what behaviour is acceptable and refusing to participate in toxic conversations, we protect ourselves from emotional harm.

3.   Cultivating   Emotional   Intelligence: Responding Thoughtfully

Developing emotional intelligence allows us to respond thoughtfully to toxic situations rather than reacting emotionally. Understanding our emotions and those of others helps us to navigate conflicts more effectively.

4. Encouraging Open Communication: Fostering a Safe Space

Promoting open and honest communication creates a safe atmosphere where people feel comfortable expressing their feelings and concerns. Encourage others to share their experiences and offer help when needed.

5. Addressing Toxic Behaviour: Confronting the Issue

It's important to address toxic behaviour directly and assertively. Engaging in constructive conversations can help raise awareness about the effect of negative behaviours and support change.

6. Promoting Empathy and Understanding: Building Connections

Encouraging empathy and understanding helps people connect on a deeper level. Understanding each other's views can bridge gaps and reduce conflicts.

7. Providing Resources and Support: Offering Help for Change

Toxicity can sometimes emerge from personal struggles or unaddressed issues. Providing resources such as counselling or workshops can help people in their journey to change negative behaviours.

8. Encouraging Positive Feedback: Reinforcing Positive Actions

Positive reinforcement encourages individuals to continue showing constructive behaviour. Acknowledge and appreciate good actions, no matter how small they may seem.

9. Avoiding Toxic Environments: Choosing Wisely

When possible, distance yourself from toxic environments or interactions. Surrounding yourself with positive influences can have a significant effect on your well-being.

10. Practising Self-Care: Prioritising Your Well-Being

Prioritising self-care is important in countering toxicity. Engaging in activities that promote relaxation and positivity can help keep mental balance.

11. Being Accountable: Reflecting on Our Own Actions

It's important to be accountable for our own behaviour and how it may affect others. Reflect on your actions and strive to add positively to the environment around you.

12. Leading by Example: Influencing Others Positively

Lead by example by showing empathy, respect, and constructive communication. Your actions can influence others to follow suit and add to a healthier environment.

In conclusion, countering toxicity includes recognizing negative behaviours, setting limits, and promoting positive interactions. By supporting open communication, empathy, and constructive feedback, we can create environments where people feel valued, supported, and encouraged to grow. Countering toxicity is not a one-time effort but a continuous commitment to spreading positivity and nurturing healthy relationships in our personal and work lives. Ultimately, it is through collective efforts that we can build a world free from toxicity, where people can thrive and reach their full potential.

CHAPTER EIGHT

Leadership's Role in Addressing Work Jerks and Creating a Respectful Environment

As the driving force behind organisational culture, leadership plays a crucial role in addressing work jerks and creating a respectful and positive work environment. When toxic behaviours go unaddressed, they can erode trust, hamper teamwork, and reduce employee happiness. Effective leaders realise the importance of confronting work jerks and actively work towards promoting an atmosphere of respect, empathy, and inclusivity. By setting clear expectations, leading by example, and implementing suitable policies, leaders can create a workplace where all employees feel valued and supported.

1. Setting Clear Expectations: Defining Workplace Norms

Effective leaders set the tone for workplace behaviour by establishing clear expectations and beliefs. They explain a zero-tolerance policy for toxic behaviours, ensuring that employees understand the consequences of engaging in such conduct.

2. Addressing Issues Promptly: Nipping Problems in the Bud

When toxic behaviours emerge, leaders must address them promptly and openly. By addressing issues early on, leaders prevent them from escalating and show their commitment to maintaining a respectful environment.

3. Promoting Open Communication: Encouraging Honest Feedback

Creating a culture of open communication allows employees to voice their worries without fear of reprisal. Leaders who actively seek feedback and listen to their workers create an environment where issues can be addressed proactively.

4. Leading by Example: Modeling Positive Behavior

Leaders must embody the behaviours they expect from their workers. By showing empathy, respect, and professionalism, leaders set a powerful example for others to follow.

5. Implementing Conflict Resolution Training: Equipping Employees with Skills

Providing conflict resolution training for employees equips them with the skills to handle difficult interactions, including those with work jerks. This training fosters constructive communication and helps build stronger teams.

6. Fostering Empathy and Understanding: Building a Supportive Culture

Empathetic leaders cultivate an environment where workers feel understood and supported. Leaders who prioritise empathy create stronger relationships and add to a more cohesive and harmonious workplace.

7. Recognizing Positive Behavior: Reinforcing Respectful Actions

Recognizing and celebrating good behaviour reinforces the value of respectful interactions. Leaders who acknowledge employees' efforts to keep a respectful environment urge others to follow suit.

8. Implementing Reporting Mechanisms: Ensuring a Safe Environment

Leaders should establish anonymous reporting mechanisms for workers to voice concerns about toxic behaviours. Providing a safe space for reporting allows employees to share their experiences without fear of retaliation.

9. Promoting Inclusivity and Diversity: Embracing Differences

Inclusive leaders build environments that embrace diversity and value different views. By promoting inclusivity, leaders promote creativity and innovation within their teams.

10. Holding Everyone Accountable: Consistency in Enforcement

Leaders must hold all employees accountable for their actions, regardless of their place within the organisation. Consistency in enforcing policies gives a message that toxic behaviours are unacceptable.

11. Providing Support and Resources: Assisting Personal Development

Leaders should provide tools and support for workers who exhibit toxic behaviours and show a willingness to change. This assistance can add to their personal development and growth.

12. Evaluating and Adapting: Continuous Improvement

Effective leaders constantly evaluate the work environment and adapt their strategies as needed to keep a respectful and positive culture. They are open to feedback and constantly seek ways to improve the workplace.

In conclusion, leadership's part in addressing work jerks and building a respectful environment is pivotal in shaping the organisational culture. Leaders set the standards for workplace behaviour, handle issues promptly, and promote open communication. By leading by example, promoting empathy, and adopting appropriate policies, leaders can create a workplace where all employees feel respected, valued, and supported. A respectful environment leads to increased employee satisfaction, improved teamwork, and eventually adds to the organisation's overall success.

CHAPTER NINE

Recognizing and Handling Passive-Aggressive Work Jerks

Dealing with passive-aggressive work jerks can be particularly challenging due to their indirect and often subtle approach to showing hostility or discontent. Passive-aggressive people may mask their true feelings and intentions behind sarcasm, backhanded compliments, or avoiding direct confrontation. Recognizing and handling passive-aggressive behaviour is crucial for keeping a healthy work environment and fostering effective communication. By staying aware of the signs, addressing the behaviour directly, and promoting open dialogue, we can handle interactions with passive-aggressive work jerks with assertiveness and integrity.

1. Recognizing Passive-Aggressive Behaviour: Identifying the Signs

Passive-aggressive behaviour can appear in various ways, including silent treatment, sarcasm, gossip, or procrastination. Recognizing these signs is the first step in addressing the problem effectively.

2. Avoiding Assumptions: Seeking Clarity

When confronted with possible passive-aggressive behaviour, avoid making assumptions about the individual's motives. Seek clarity by tackling the action directly and asking for explanations.

3. Staying Calm and Composed: Emotional Regulation

Dealing with passive-aggressive individuals can be frustrating, but keeping composure is important. Emotional regulation allows you to react thoughtfully and avoid escalating conflicts.

4. Directly Addressing the Behavior: Open Communication

Engage in open and direct communication with the passive-aggressive person. Express your worries about their behaviour and how it affects the work environment.

5. Using "I" Statements: Expressing Your Feelings

When addressing passive-aggressive behaviour, use "I" statements to share your thoughts and observations without sounding accusatory. This method encourages more constructive dialogue.

6. Seeking Feedback: Encouraging Honest Communication

Encourage the passive-aggressive individual to share their viewpoint and feelings about the situation. Seeking feedback can help find underlying issues and potential resolutions.

7. Setting Boundaries: Defining Acceptable Behaviour

Clearly explain your boundaries and standards regarding respectful communication and teamwork. Setting limits can help deter passive-aggressive behaviour.

8. Offering Constructive Feedback: Encouraging Positive Change

Provide constructive feedback on specific instances of passive-aggressive behaviour and offer ideas for more appropriate ways to communicate.

9. Documenting Incidents: Keeping a Record

Keeping a record of passive-aggressive incidents can be useful if further action or intervention becomes necessary. Document dates, times, and details to provide context.

10. Involving Mediation if Needed: Seeking Objective Help

If addressing the passive-aggressive behaviour directly doesn't give desired results, consider involving a neutral third party, such as a mediator or supervisor, to facilitate the conversation.

11. Focusing on Professionalism: Avoiding Emotional Reactions

Responding to passive-aggressive behaviour with emotional responses can fuel the situation. Stay focused on professionalism and constructive dialogue.

12. Knowing When to Disengage: Prioritising Your Well-Being

If the passive-aggressive behaviour persists despite your efforts, recognize when it's best to disengage briefly and seek support from colleagues or supervisors.

In conclusion, spotting and handling passive-aggressive work jerks require vigilance, open communication, and emotional regulation. By identifying the signs of passive-aggressive behaviour, addressing it openly, and promoting constructive dialogue, we can navigate interactions with these people while upholding our professionalism and integrity. Remember that handling passive-aggressive behaviour requires patience and assertiveness, but by prioritising a healthy work environment and effective communication, we can create a workplace where respect and open conversation thrive.

CHAPTER TEN

Stress Management:

Coping with Work Jerks' Impact on Your Well-Being

Dealing with work jerks in the workplace can take a toll on your emotional well-being and general job satisfaction. The negative effect of their behaviour may lead to stress, anxiety, and even feelings of inadequacy. Coping with work jerks' effect on your well-being takes resilience, self-awareness, and proactive self-care strategies. By prioritising your mental health, setting boundaries, and getting help, you can navigate these challenging situations while preserving your emotional balance and professional growth.

1. Acknowledge Your Feelings: Validating Your Emotions

Recognize that it's normal to feel upset or frustrated when dealing with work jerks. Acknowledging your emotions helps validate your feelings and allows you to address them effectively.

2. Practice Self-Awareness: Understanding Your Triggers

Cultivate self-awareness to find the specific triggers that affect your well-being. Understanding what situations or actions impact you the most empowers you to develop coping strategies.

3. Set Boundaries: Protecting Your Emotional Space

Establish clear boundaries with work jerks to protect your mental well-being. Politely but firmly communicate your limits and expectations, ensuring that you maintain a sense of control in difficult circumstances.

4. Focus on What You Can Control: Letting Go of the Rest

Accept that you cannot control the behaviour of work jerks, but you can control your own reactions and answers. Focus on managing your responses rather than trying to change their behaviour.

5. Practise Emotional Regulation: Managing Stress and Anxiety

Engage in techniques such as deep breathing, meditation, or exercise to handle stress and anxiety caused by interactions with work jerks. Emotional regulation can help you keep composure during challenging moments.

6. Seek Emotional Support: Sharing with Trusted Colleagues

Connect with trusted colleagues who understand your position and can provide empathy and support. Talking about your experiences with others can be healing and validating.

7. Utilise Resources: Employee Assistance Programs and Counseling

If possible, take advantage of employee assistance programs or counselling services offered by your organisation. These resources offer professional help to cope with workplace stress.

8. Engage in Positive Coping Mechanisms: Hobbies and Activities

Participate in hobbies, activities, or interests outside of work to unwind and lower stress. Engaging in enjoyable hobbies can provide a sense of fulfilment and help you detach from work-related stressors.

9. Focus on Your Strengths: Building Confidence

Recognize your strengths and accomplishments, reminding yourself of your worth in the workplace. Building confidence in your abilities can counteract the negative effect of work jerks' behaviour.

10. Develop a Support Network: Surrounding Yourself with Positivity

Create a support network of friends and family who can offer encouragement and viewpoint outside of work. Having a positive impact can boost your resilience and general well-being.

11. Engage in Mindfulness: Staying Present and Grounded

Practice mindfulness to stay present in the moment and centred. Being mindful helps you manage negative thoughts and emotions, allowing you to react thoughtfully to challenging situations.

12. Consider Seeking New Opportunities: Prioritising Your Growth

If the impact of work jerks on your well-being becomes overwhelming, consider exploring new job opportunities that fit with your values and offer a healthier work environment.

In conclusion, coping with work jerks' impact on your well-being takes a combination of self-awareness, resilience, and proactive self-care strategies. Recognizing your emotions, setting boundaries, and seeking emotional support are crucial for keeping your emotional balance in challenging work environments. Prioritising your well-being and adopting coping mechanisms can help you navigate interactions with work jerks while preserving your mental health and professional growth. Remember that you deserve to work in a workplace that values respect and positivity, and taking steps to protect your well-being is a testament to your self-worth and resilience.

CHAPTER ELEVEN

Cooperation Tactics:

Strengthening Unity in the Face of Work pulls

Dealing with work pulls in the plant can beget pressure and disrupt platoon dynamics. still, rather of letting their geste
peak and demoralise the platoon, it's important to concentrate on strengthening concinnity. By

creating a culture of collaboration, empathy, and adaptability, brigades can navigate challenges together and minimise the negative impact of work pulls. Emphasising participating pretensions, open communication, and support for one another can help make a united front that thrives indeed in the face of tough personalities.

1. Emphasise Shared pretensions fastening on Common objects

pressing the platoon's participating pretensions and objects provides a sense of purpose and concinnity. Remind platoon members that they're working towards a common thing, encouraging them to support one another despite challenges.

2. Promote Open Communication Encouraging Honest Dialogue

Encourage open and transparent dialogue among platoon members. A culture of open communication allows individualities to express their enterprises about work pulls' geste
, fostering a probative atmosphere.

3. Build Trust and Empathy Understanding Each Other's Perspectives

Strengthen platoon concinnity by erecting trust and understanding among members. Encourage platoon members to understand and support one another, creating a feeling of fellowship and collective respect.

4. Address Conflicts Collaboratively Seeking Formative results

When conflicts appear due to work pulls, address them collaboratively. Involve all platoon members in chancing results, which can lead to further effective judgments and produce a sense of power in the issues.

5. Fete and Celebrate benefactions buttressing Team sweats

Acknowledge and celebrate individual and platoon achievements. Feting sweats and bents reinforces platoon concinnity and boosts morale.

6. Offer Support and Mentorship Strengthening Team Bonds

Encourage mentorship and help within the platoon. elderly members can guide and empower newer members, furnishing a sense of belonging and collective growth.

7. Organise Team- Building Conditioning Strengthening connections

Arrange platoon- structure events to strengthen connections and ameliorate collaboration. Conditioning that promotes cooperation and communication can help ground gaps caused by work pulls.

8. Encourage Collaborative Problem- working Empowering Team Members

Empower platoon members to join in collaborative problems- working. When people feel involved in the decision- making process, they're more likely to embrace the results as a platoon.

9. give Training and coffers Equipping the platoon

Offer disagreement resolution and communication training for the platoon. Equipping platoon members with the necessary chops to handle gruelling relations can improve their confidence and adaptability.

10. Foster a Positive Work Culture Setting the Tone from Above Leaders play a significant part in fostering platoon consistency. They should set the tone for a positive work atmosphere that emphasises collaboration and regardful communication.

11. Lead by Example Modeling Positive geste Platoon leaders should model the conduct they anticipate from their platoon members. Demonstrating empathy and respect pushes others to follow suit.

12. Celebrate Diversity and Addition Valuing Different Perspectives Grasp diversity and equivalency within the platoon. Fete and admire the unique strengths

and perspectives that each platoon member brings to the table.

In conclusion, strengthening concinnity in the face of work pulls collaborative trouble from the entire platoon. By emphasising participating pretensions, promoting open communication, and erecting trust and empathy, brigades can navigate obstacles together and maintain their sense of purpose and morale. Leaders play a pivotal part in fostering a positive work culture and leading by illustration. Through cooperation, collective support, and a commitment to regardful communication, brigades can make adaptability and minimise the negative effect of work pulls. By fastening on concinnity, brigades can thrive and overcome obstacles, icing a more cohesive and productive work terrain for all.

CHAPTER TWELVE

Turning Challenges into Opportunities:

Lessons from Success Stories

Success stories inspire and motivate us, giving valuable lessons that we can apply to our own lives and pursuits. Whether it's in business, sports, personal achievements, or overcoming obstacles, success stories offer insights and wisdom that can guide us on our own paths to success. Here are some general lessons we can learn from success stories:

1. Perseverance and Resilience: Many success stories highlight the value of perseverance and resilience in the face of obstacles. Successful individuals often encounter setbacks and failures, but they keep moving forward, learning from their mistakes, and adapting their strategies.

2. Vision and Goal making: Success stories emphasise the power of having a clear vision and making specific goals. Having a well-defined direction and purpose guides one's actions and choices, leading to greater focus and determination.

3. Passion and Dedication: Successful people are often deeply passionate about what they do. Their dedication and love for their work drive them to go above and beyond, putting in the extra effort needed to achieve their goals.

4. Continuous Learning and Growth: Success stories show the importance of continuous learning and personal growth. Successful individuals spend time acquiring new knowledge, seeking feedback, and improving their skills.

5. Embracing Failure as a Learning Opportunity: Failure is a natural part of the road to success. Successful people view failures as opportunities for growth and learning, rather than as reasons to give up.

6. Taking Calculated Risks: Success often means taking calculated risks. Success stories teach us that calculated risks can lead to significant benefits, and that being too risk-averse can hold us back from reaching our full potential.

7. Surrounding Yourself with the Right People: The company we keep can greatly influence our success. Successful individuals surround themselves with helpful, motivated, and positive people who inspire and uplift them.

8. Respecting Time Management: Success stories highlight the worth of effective time management. Successful individuals prioritise tasks, set deadlines, and avoid time-wasting activities to maximise output.

9. Staying Humble and thankful: Success stories remind us to remain humble and thankful for our achievements. Recognizing the contributions of others and expressing gratitude promotes positive relationships and opens doors for future opportunities.

10. Embracing flexibility: Flexibility and flexibility are key traits found in success stories. Successful individuals are open to change and ready to adapt their strategies as circumstances evolve.

11. Overcoming Self-Doubt: Success stories often involve individuals who faced self-doubt and phoney syndrome. Overcoming these

internal obstacles and believing in oneself is important for achieving success.

12. Giving Back and Making a Difference: Many success stories involve individuals who give back to their communities or help to causes they are passionate about. Success is often more important when it positively impacts others' lives.

In conclusion, success stories offer a wealth of important lessons that can guide us on our own journeys to success. From perseverance and resilience to vision and goal setting, these stories teach us the value of passion, dedication, and continuous learning. Embracing failure, taking calculated risks, and surrounding ourselves with the right people can greatly influence our path to success. Practising effective time management, staying humble and grateful, and being adaptable are also essential traits found in successful people. Overcoming self-doubt and giving back to others are powerful messages that remind us of the profound effect of success on both personal and communal levels. By learning from these lessons and applying them to our lives, we can increase our chances of achieving our goals and living happy and successful lives.

CHAPTER THIRTEEN

Mediation and Intervention:

Facilitating Dialogue to Address Work Jerks

Addressing work jerks in the workplace takes open and honest dialogue. Facilitating conversations helps team members to express their concerns, understand one another's perspectives, and work collaboratively to find constructive solutions. By fostering a safe and respectful environment for dialogue, organisations can effectively address work jerk behaviour, promote understanding, and develop a culture of respect and cooperation.

1. Create a Safe Space: Establishing Trust

Start by making a safe and confidential space for dialogue. Ensure that all team members feel safe expressing their worries without fear of retaliation or judgement.

2. Set Clear Objectives: Defining the Purpose

Clearly define the goals of the dialogue session. Whether it is to address specific incidents or improve team dynamics, having a clear purpose helps keep the talk focused and productive.

3. Choose a Neutral Facilitator: Promoting Fairness

In situations where tensions are high, consider involving a neutral facilitator, such as an HR professional or mediator, to lead the talk. A neutral facilitator can ensure fairness and guide the talk towards resolution.

4. Encourage Active Listening: Valuing Each Perspective

Emphasise the value of active listening during the dialogue session. Encourage participants to listen attentively to one another's worries and perspectives, valuing each person's input.

5. Use "I" Statements: Promoting Non-Defensive Communication

Encourage participants to use "I" statements when expressing their thoughts and worries. This method promotes non-defensive communication and avoids blame.

6. Address Specific Incidents: Focusing on Behavior

Address specific incidents of work jerk behaviour during the conversation. Focus on the behaviour rather than personal attacks to keep a constructive tone.

7. Seek to Understand Motivations: Uncovering Root Causes

Encourage participants to explore the reasons behind work jerk behaviour. Understanding the underlying reasons can help find answers that address root causes.

8. Identify Shared Goals: Finding Common Ground

Look for shared goals and hobbies among team members. Identifying common ground can promote a sense of unity and encourage collaboration.

9. Brainstorm Solutions: Collaborating for Resolution

Engage all participants in brainstorming possible solutions. Encourage creativity and openness to try various approaches to address the problem.

10. Establish Action Steps: Committing to Change

After identifying potential solutions, set clear action steps to address the work jerk behaviour.

Assign tasks and set timelines for implementing changes.

11. Implement Follow-Up: Ensuring Accountability

Schedule follow-up meetings to monitor progress and assess the effectiveness of the solutions implemented. Regular check-ins ensure accountability and provide a chance to make further adjustments if necessary.

12. Promote a Culture of Respect: Sustaining Positive Dialogue

Beyond individual dialogue sessions, support an ongoing culture of respect and open communication in the workplace. Encourage regular team meetings and places where concerns can be addressed constructively.

In conclusion, facilitating dialogue to address work jerks is a critical step towards creating a respectful and cooperative work environment. By creating a safe place for open communication, setting clear objectives, and promoting active listening, teams can address work jerk behaviour and resolve conflicts successfully. Engaging a neutral facilitator can provide extra help and ensure fairness in the process. During the dialogue, addressing specific incidents, trying to understand motivations, and identifying shared goals can promote mutual understanding and collaboration. Brainstorming solutions and establishing action steps guarantee that the dialogue leads to actionable change. By promoting a culture of respect and ongoing communication, organisations can sustain positive dialogue and handle work jerk behaviour proactively, eventually creating a more harmonious and productive work environment for all team members.

CHAPTER FOURTEEN

Legal Considerations:

When Workplace Conflict Requires Professional Assistance

Workplace conflict is an essential aspect of organisational dynamics, but in some cases, conflicts can escalate to a point where professional assistance becomes necessary. When conflicts are left unaddressed or attempts to resolve them internally prove ineffective, finding external help can be crucial to prevent further escalation and to restore a healthy work environment. Professional assistance, in the form of mediation and intervention, can bring a fresh perspective, promote open communication, and enable constructive resolution.

1. Escalation of Conflict: Signs to Look Out For

Recognizing the signs of escalating conflict is important. These signs may include increased tension, frequent disagreements, reduced output, employee disengagement, and a toxic work environment.

2. Exhaustion of Internal Efforts: When Internal Resolution Fails

If internal attempts to address the conflict, such as meetings or informal discussions, fail to yield good results, seeking external assistance may be necessary to break the impasse.

3. Involvement of Multiple Parties: Managing Complexity

When conflicts involve multiple parties or departments, they become more complex to settle. Professional assistance can provide unbiased mediation to ensure all views are heard and considered.

4. Employee Well-Being Affected: Prioritising Mental Health

If workplace conflict starts to impact employee well-being, resulting in stress, anxiety, or reduced job satisfaction, getting professional assistance is vital to protect mental health.

5. High-Profile Conflicts: Addressing Sensitive Issues

High-profile conflicts involving senior management or key personnel may require professional intervention to keep confidentiality and address sensitive issues successfully.

6. Repeated Pattern of Conflict: Breaking Unhealthy Cycles

When conflicts recur or follow a pattern, expert assistance can help identify underlying issues and break unhealthy cycles, leading to more sustainable resolutions.

7. Communication Breakdown: Facilitating Dialogue

Professional mediators can help facilitate open and constructive dialogue between conflicting groups. Their neutrality can create a safe place for expressing concerns and finding common ground.

8. Restoring Trust: Building Bridges

In highly conflicted situations where trust has been eroded, intervention by a neutral third party can be instrumental in rebuilding trust and encouraging reconciliation.

9. Leveraging Conflict as an Opportunity: Transforming Challenges

Skilled mediators can help parties view conflict as a chance for growth and positive change rather than solely a source of tension.

10. Confidentiality: Protecting Privacy

External mediators ensure confidentiality during the intervention process, allowing workers to feel safe discussing sensitive issues without fear of repercussions.

11. Objective Insights: Gaining Fresh Perspectives

Professional mediators offer objective insights into the conflict, unburdened by pre-existing biases or personal stakes, allowing them to identify potential solutions that may not have been considered before.

12. Empowering the Workforce: Encouraging Ownership

Engaging in professional mediation enables employees to take ownership of the resolution process. This can lead to more sustainable outcomes and greater commitment to positive change.

In conclusion, when workplace conflicts become too complex or remain unresolved despite internal efforts, finding professional assistance through mediation and intervention is a proactive step to address the issues effectively.

External assistance can provide fresh views, facilitate open communication, and empower the workforce to take ownership of the resolution process. Involving neutral third parties can also protect confidentiality, especially in high-profile or sensitive fights. By recognizing the signs of escalating conflicts and prioritising employee well-being, organisations can effectively address workplace conflicts and create a more harmonious and productive work environment for all.

CHAPTER FIFTEEN

Transitioning and Moving On:

Evaluating Your Career Choices in the Face of Work Jerks

Dealing with work jerks in the workplace can have a significant effect on your career satisfaction and overall well-being. When faced with a toxic work environment, it becomes crucial to evaluate your career choices and consider whether staying in such a situation fits with your long-term goals and values. Evaluating your job choices in the face of work jerks includes reflecting on the impact of the toxic environment, exploring alternatives, and making decisions that prioritise your personal growth and well-being.

1. Assessing the Impact on Your Well-Being: Recognizing the Toll

Reflect on how the toxic work atmosphere is affecting your emotional and mental well-being. Consider issues such as stress, anxiety, job satisfaction, and work-life balance.

2. Identifying Triggers and Coping Mechanisms: Understanding Your Responses

Identify specific triggers that worsen the effect of work jerks on your well-being. Understand your coping mechanisms and whether they successfully address the stress caused by the situation.

3. Reflecting on Your Career Goals: Aligning with Your Aspirations

Evaluate whether your present career path aligns with your long-term goals and aspirations. Determine if staying in a toxic setting is hindering your career growth and development.

4. Weighing Pros and Cons: Considering the Trade-offs

List the pros and cons of staying in the current job versus exploring other career opportunities. Assess the possible benefits and drawbacks of both options.

5. Seeking Internal Solutions: Exploring Change Within the Organization

Consider if there are opportunities for change within the company. Discuss concerns with management or human resources and explore if changes can improve the work environment.

6. Exploring Career Transitions: Pursuing New Paths

If staying in the current role seems unsustainable, explore other career opportunities that fit better with your values and professional goals.

7. Networking and Skill Development: Preparing for Change

Network with professionals in your field of interest and engage in skill development activities to prepare for potential job transitions.

8. Seeking Support from Colleagues: Sharing Experiences

Connect with colleagues who may be facing similar challenges. Sharing experiences can provide useful insights and emotional support.

9. Evaluating Company Culture: Considering Organisational Values

Assess the company's mindset and values to determine if the toxic behaviour is an isolated incident or indicative of systemic problems.

10. Consulting with Career Counsellors: Seeking Expert Advice

Consult with career counsellors or coaches who can provide advice and support during the decision-making process.

11. Evaluating Financial Implications: Considering Practical Aspects

Consider the financial implications of job transitions or possible periods of unemployment. Make informed choices considering practical aspects.

12. Trusting Your Instincts: Prioritising Your Well-Being

Trust your instincts and make choices that prioritise your well-being and personal growth. Your happiness and career satisfaction should be paramount factors.

In conclusion, evaluating your career choices in the face of work jerks is an important step towards prioritising your well-being and professional growth. Reflect on the effect of the toxic environment, explore alternatives, and weigh the pros and cons of different options.

Seek internal solutions, explore job transitions, and consider the company's culture and values. Engage in networking and skill development to prepare for possible changes, and seek support from colleagues and career counsellors. Ultimately, prioritise your personal well-being and trust your instincts when making job choices. Remember that your career journey is a path of growth and fulfilment, and making choices that fit with your values and goals will lead to greater job satisfaction and professional success in the long run.

CHAPTER SIXTEEN

Success Stories:

Overcoming Work Jerk Challenges

Dealing with work jerks in the workplace can be mentally draining and demotivating. Their negative behaviour can create a toxic work atmosphere, affecting productivity, job satisfaction, and general well-being. However, with the right strategies and mindset, it is possible to face work jerk challenges and keep your resilience and empowerment. Here are some successful strategies to navigate these difficult situations:

1. Stay Calm and Composed: Emotional Regulation

When faced with work jerks, staying calm and composed is important. Practise emotional regulation methods like deep breathing or mindfulness to handle stress and avoid reacting impulsively.

2. Set Boundaries: Protecting Your Space

Establish clear limits with work jerks to protect yourself from their negative influence. Communicate assertively when you feel uncomfortable and demand your right to a respectful work environment.

3. Focus on What You Can Control: Letting Go of the Rest

While you cannot control the behaviour of work jerks, you can control your reactions and answers. Focus on aspects of your work and life that you can control and affect positively.

4. Seek Support from Colleagues: Strength in Numbers

Connect with colleagues who may be facing similar challenges. Sharing experiences and giving support can help you feel less isolated and empower you to handle the situation better.

5. Document Incidents: Keeping a Record

Keep a record of any instances of work jerk behaviour you experience. Document dates, times, and specifics to provide context and proof if needed in the future.

6. Engage in Positive Coping Mechanisms: Stress Relief

Engage in hobbies, exercise, or other things that bring you joy and help relieve stress. Taking care of your well-being outside of work can improve your resilience to work jerk problems.

7. Focus on Professionalism: Maintain Your Integrity

Regardless of how work jerks behave, keep your professionalism and integrity. Rise above their negativity and show your commitment to a positive work culture.

8. Seek Feedback and Growth Opportunities: Continuous Improvement

Request feedback from managers and colleagues to identify areas of improvement. Use challenges as chances for personal growth and development.

9. Engage in Conflict Resolution Training: Building Skills

Participate in conflict resolution training to build effective communication and negotiation skills. These skills can be useful when dealing with work jerk challenges.

10. Assess Long-Term Career Goals: Evaluating Your Path

Evaluate whether the current workplace fits with your long-term career goals and values. If work jerk challenges persist and impede your growth, consider exploring other career possibilities.

11. Utilise Employee Assistance Programs: Support Services

If your company offers employee assistance programs, take advantage of counselling or support services to help you cope with work jerk challenges.

12. Know When to Seek External Help: Professional Mediation

If work jerk challenges continue and significantly affect your well-being, consider seeking external help, such as professional mediation or intervention, to address the situation effectively.

In conclusion, overcoming work jerk challenges takes a mix of emotional resilience, assertiveness, and support. Stay composed, set limits, and focus on what you can control. Seek support from colleagues, participate in positive coping mechanisms, and keep your professionalism. Document incidents and seek comments for personal growth. Assess your long-term job goals and consider seeking external help if necessary. Remember that work jerk challenges are not a reflection of your worth or skills. Empower yourself by taking proactive steps to protect your well-being, keep your professionalism, and explore opportunities for personal growth and development. By employing these strategies, you can handle work jerk challenges with strength, resilience, and empowerment, ensuring a more positive work experience and contributing to a healthier workplace environment for yourself and your coworkers